Body Language

Attract, Influence, and Understand how to Communicate with people around, non-verbal

Table Of Contents

Introduction-

Body language is a universal unspoken language, that we all speak but have no control over. It is the language of truth, one that cannot tell a lie.

It is a language that if you understand it properly if you learn how to read it, you are going to begin to not only understand other people better but yourself as well.

Studies have found that up to 55 percent of our communication is nonverbal, which means that it is done through body language. Wouldn't you like to know what is being said to you?

By learning how to read body language, you will be able to tell when someone has come to a decision before they even say anything. You will be able to know how someone feels about you and if they are being truthful with you.

Learning how to read body language is going to help you learn how to communicate with many different types of people, ask smarter questions and know when you have discussed a topic that is sensitive.

Of course, when you are in a crowd or even a meeting at work, there are always going to be those people who just don't speak up, but learning how to read their body language is going to enable you to understand just what they are feeling and thinking.

You can use body language to your advantage in every area of your life. From being able to tell if your children are being honest with you, to observing how your boss really feels about your ideas, and even to understand if that person you are interested in, might be feeling the same way.

Imagine how different your life would be if you could always tell how someone was really feeling or if they were being honest with you! Imagine how different you would phrase your words if you knew exactly how they were affecting the people that you were communicating with!

That is exactly what this book is going to teach you. From beginning to end, you will learn how to read body language so that you are able to better communicate with those around you.

Chapter 1- Body Language Top To Bottom

We use body language every single day and we use each and every part of our body to communicate. Body language is not something most people have any control over. It is something that happens, no matter how hard we try to stop it. Body language is an automatic response to how we feel and what we are thinking.

I want to begin by talking about body language in general and common types of body language. Later in the book, we will go into more detail, discussing the difference between men and women when it comes to body language, romantic body language, learning how to control your body language and even how body language is used in different cultures.

For now, I want to begin by talking about your face. Most people do not understand just how much the face is used when it comes to body language, but there is a lot of information to be gained if you just spend some time watching a person's face.

Let's begin by talking about the color of the face. There is no way for anyone to control the color of their face and this is a great way to begin understanding how someone is feeling.

If the face is redder than normal, there are a few things that could be causing this. It is up to you to determine the situation and decide what is causing the reddening of the face.

Of course, the first thing that comes to mind when you see someone whose face is a bit red is that they are hot. This can be caused by the temperature in the room or if they have been exercising. However, when it comes to body language, a red face may mean that the person is angry.

This is usually the first sign of anger and a sign that you should watch for when you are discussing sensitive topics.

A red face can also be a sign that the person is embarrassed. This is also something that you need to watch for, especially if you are joking with someone and are not sure how they feel about it.

If you notice that the face is much whiter than normal, there could be a few reasons for this. First, you want to rule out being cold. When a person is cold, they tend to have a whiter complexion than when they are warm.

This could also mean that the person is suffering from extreme fear. Have you ever noticed the way a person's color seems to drain out of them when they are afraid?

Being whiter than normal could also indicate that the person is not feeling well. This is good to know, especially when it comes to people who are generally unwell.

You might notice that the person that you are communicating is sweating a bit. In this case, it could be caused by the heat, which you will want to rule out. Once heat is ruled out, you can determine if the sweat is because the person is excited, fearful or if they are dealing with a build-up of emotions.

Now, let's talk a bit about how you can determine emotions when looking at the face.

If a person is dealing with anxiety, you might find that they have their brow wrinkled, their lower lip may tremble and their head might be tilted down just slightly.

If the person is dealing with fear, you will notice that their eyes are either open wide, completely closed or pointed toward the ground. Their eyebrows will generally be raised, and the mouth might be open or the corners could be turned down into a frown.

The chin will be pulled into the chest, while the person has their head down, looking toward the ground and their face will usually be quite pale.

When a person is happy, you can literally see the sparkles in their eyes, they will be smiling or even laughing, they will look straight ahead, not looking up or down.

If a person is sad, they will look down, often because there are tears in their eyes. They tend to have their lips pinched together in an effort not to frown or cry and the chin may be pushed forward.

If a person is feeling envy toward you, they will stare at you, they will tend to have a frown on their face and they will tend to scoff at you.

When a person is looking at you with desire, you might find that their eyes are wide open and that their pupils are dilated. One or both eyebrows might be slightly raised and their lips will be parted ever so slightly. They may also tilt their head forward.

If a person is interested in what you are saying, they will look at you, without looking away, possibly even squinting. Their lips will generally be pressed together and their head will be erect.

When a person is suffering from boredom, they tend to look away from the person that they are communicating with. The corner of the lips might be pulled to one side and they may rest their head on one or both of their hands.

A surprised person will have wide open eyes, their eyebrows might be raised, and the mouth will generally be open.

When a person is feeling disgusted, they tend to not only turn their eyes, but their head away from the object of their disgust as well. The nostrils will generally be flared, the nose might be twisted and the mouth will be closed.

As you can see, a lot of information can be collected if we just pay attention to the faces of the people that we are speaking with.

Next up is the hands. When a person is sitting with their hand open, palm up, it means that they are accepting of the person they are speaking with or the idea that is being discussed. It is a sign that the person trusts you.

If a person touches you with their hand, it means that they are familiar with you or that they are fond of you.

If, however, the hand is closed, it means that the person is feeling uncomfortable, possibly trying to reassure themselves, they feel defensive, agitated or are seeking to control the situation.

When the arms are open, it shows that the person is trusting, they agree with you or the situation, or they are showing excitement. If the arms are crossed, however, the person is protecting their core which means that they feel threatened, are tense, do not agree with you or are feeling rejected.

When the legs are crossed, it is much like when the arms are crossed, the person is trying to protect themselves, or distance themselves from others because they feel threatened. The person may be dealing with insecurities or feeling closed off.

When the legs are spread out, however, this is showing confidence. If the legs are pointed in one direction it may show that the person is interested in whatever or whoever the legs are pointed at.

If the person is sitting on the edge of their seat, it means that they are full of passion and ready to start taking action.

This is the basics of body language, however, it needs to be looked at in context with the situation. If a person is sitting with their arms crossed, it does not always mean that they are disengaged, it may mean that the room is too cold and they are simply trying to keep warm.

If a person is resting their head on their hands, it does not always mean that they are bored, especially if it is three in the morning and the two of you have been talking all night.

You cannot simply focus on how the body moves in hopes of

understanding body language, but instead, you must pay attention to outside factors as well.

Chapter 2- Romantic Body Language

Reading the signs of attraction is one of the reasons that so many people become interested in body language. They want to know for sure if someone is romantically attracted to them before they make a move and why not?

The truth is, by learning how to read body language properly, you can easily tell if the person you are interested in is interested in you.

Let's begin with men. Men like women cannot hide the fact that they are attracted to you if you know how to read their body language. Let's begin with the man's face.

If a man is interested in you, then he will have his eyebrows raised even if it is just slightly. When you look him in the eyes, his lips will part, however, you must be paying attention because it could just be by a small amount.

If the man is looking at you and smiling, chances are that he is interested in you. In order to be sure that he is not just being nice, pay attention to his nostrils. If they flare slightly, he is romantically attracted.

Grooming is another thing that you will want to look for. Just like a woman will straighten her hair or make sure that her clothes are straightened out on her body, a man will subconsciously groom himself.

You might find that he is running his fingers through is

hair, or straightening it depending on the haircut he has, or that he is adjusting his tie or jacket.

Just like you will play with your hair or necklace, if a man is attracted to you, then he might play with the buttons on his shirt or touch his face.

Standing erect with his hands on his hips in almost a Superman pose is one way that men try to get you to notice them. If he is sitting, his legs are going to be far apart, showing that he is confident.

When it comes to touching, many women wonder if the man they are interested in is touching them because he is interested or because they are friends. Here is how to tell. If a man is touching you on the elbow, or on the small of your back, he is interested in you romantically.

However, even if he is not touching you, there is no need to worry. He might just be shy. This is why it is important for you to pay attention to the other types of body language that signal physical attraction.

Now it is time to let the gentlemen know how to read a woman's body language. If a woman is interested in you, she is not just going to check you out from afar, but she is going to make sure that you know she is doing it.

If you notice her looking at you and she looks you in the eyes for a few seconds before looking away or lowering her gaze SHE IS INTERESTED. Act now, do not wait! This is a sure sign of romantic interest.

As cliché as it might sound, if a woman is batting her eyelashes at you, she is interested. When a woman is interested in a man, she naturally blinks faster. This is what has become known as batting her eyelashes. However, what most men do not understand is that a woman has no control over this and it is a simple way to tell whether or not she is interested in you.

When a woman is interested in a man, she will bite at her lips without realizing what she is doing. This is her way of bringing your attention to her lips. She wants to feel your lips against hers!

It is important to be aware that if a woman is sitting back in her seat with her arms crossed, there is a very low chance that she is interested in you. In fact, chances are that she is uninterested and quite bored.

However, if she reaches out and touches you on the hand or arm but quickly brings her hand back to her chest, it is a sure sign she is interested.

Paying attention to the way a woman touches her hair is very important as well. For example, if she is caressing her hair, running her fingers through it or twirling it around her finger, she might be interested.

On the other hand, if her movements are jerky, it is highly likely that she is feeling uncomfortable. However, all is not lost. If you find that she is showing signs of feeling uncomfortable, simply back off a little bit. You might be coming on a bit too strong for her taste.

Pay close attention to what a woman is doing with her hands. If she is touching her lips, neck or collar bone a lot, it is a sure sign that she is attracted to you. If she is fiddling with her jewelry, there is a very high chance that she is interested.

You see, when a woman is interested in a man and she is around him, her heart beats faster, causing her to feel more energy flowing through her body. In order to control this extra energy, she will play with jewelry, her hair, and even her clothes.

On top of all of this, if you want to make sure that she is interested, watch and see if she is mirroring your actions. If a woman is mirroring your movements, it is a subconscious act that she is not even aware of, however, it is a sure sign that she is romantically attracted to you.

Chapter 3- Men's VS Women's Body Language

No matter how much alike men and women are, the fact is that we are different in many ways. One of the ways that we are different is the way that we use body language.

One of the ways that men and women differ when it comes to body language is how they approach other people. Because most women do not like to be approached from behind, they will approach people from the front, however, while men do not like to be approached from the back as well, they do not like being approached from the front.

If you want to make a woman feel comfortable when you are approaching her, it is important to do so from the front. On the other hand, if you are approaching a man, he may feel threatened if you approach him from the front so do so from the side or an angle.

When a woman is nodding while someone is speaking to her, she is doing so to ensure the person that is speaking that she is listening. She is not telling the person that she agrees with them, but that she hears what they are saying.

On the other hand, when a man is nodding while someone is speaking, it is only because they agree with what is being said. They will never nod just to show the other person that they are listening.

This means that if you are having a conversation with a woman, it is important for you to nod, while she is speaking in order to let her know you are listening, however, when you are having a conversation with a man, it is important for you to only nod when you are in agreement with what is being said.

Touch can be used to communicate many different feelings, from control to power to romantic interest. It all depends on how the touch is used and whether it is a male or female doing the touching.

When a man pats someone on the back, this can be because they want to show that they are more powerful, much like a father patting a son on the back. However, when a woman pats someone on the back, it can be to show them love, or to show that she is concerned about them, or just to congratulate them.

It is because of reasons such as these that we need to learn how to read all of the different types of body language and not just one or two.

Beginning at a young age, women are taught how to give a lot of nonverbal encouragement, such as mm-hmm, yeah, head nodding and even just leaning forward in their seat. However, men for some reason are not taught the same things. So, the next time you ladies are speaking to a man, don't feel discouraged if you are not getting the type of nonverbal encouragement that you are used to getting from the girls, and guys, be thankful that she wants to encourage you so much.

Part of body language is the vocal tones that are used. Women, when they are under stress tend to speak in a much higher pitched voice which can be troublesome in the workplace, because they tend to sound emotional. It is for this reason that it is important for women to try and take control of the tone of their voice, keeping their vocal cords relaxed, and trying to keep their voice a bit lower when they are under stress.

Men, on the other hand, do not use as many different tones as women which tends to make them sound as if they have no emotion whatsoever.

Of course, as we learned in the last chapter when it comes to romantic body language, men and women express themselves differently.

What does this mean?

It means that when you are reading a person's body language, not only do you have to take the situation into account, but you have to take into account if they are male or female. If you are a female, you cannot assume that a man is interested in you simply because they are using the body language that you would use if you were interested in them.

Likewise, if you are a man, you cannot assume that a woman will use the same body language that you will, no matter how well she fits in with the guys.

I see online, on so many different websites that different people are asking if a certain man or a woman is interested in them. The answer is that there simply is no way for anyone to know because you are the only person that can see his or her body language and determine how they feel about you.

When you are trying to read a person's body language, it is great if you know the person. For example, if the person is always smiling, it is safe to say that just because they are smiling at you, it does not mean they are attracted to you.

On the other hand, if the person is always cold, it is safe to say that they are not sitting with their arms crossed simply because they are not interested in what you have to say to them.

It is important to understand that men and women communicate differently when they are using verbal communication as well as when they are using non-verbal communication. Women are often much better at communicating verbally and as it turns out, they are actually better when communicating non-verbally as well.

This means that if you are trying to read a man's body language, you will find that they are more likely to use hand gestures while they are talking. On the other hand, a woman will use much more subtle gestures. When you are trying to read a woman's body language, you will need to watch for small facial movements such as lowering of the bow.

Of course, there are many women out there that will use hand gestures when they are excited. When a man is talking to someone, they often prefer a bit of distance between themselves and the person they are speaking with. Women, on the other hand, have no problem with being up close and personal with the people they are communicating with.

Men prefer to face the person that they are speaking with

which makes it much easier to read their body language. Women, prefer to communicate with those that are beside them.

Men are much more likely to associate touch with sexual attraction which means that it is not common for two men to touch each other while they are communicating. Women, on the other hand, associate touch with comfort which is why it is more likely for them to touch both men and women, not associating the touch with sexuality at all.

The truth is that each of us communicates differently and many of us feel more comfortable communicating one way instead of another. For example, it might be easier for one person to talk about sensitive topics via a text message while it is easier for another person to do so face to face.

In the same way, most of us will use body language differently. For example, there are men that are very touchy and just because he touches you, it does not mean that he is falling for you. There are also women that are not as touchy feely as others, however, this does not mean that she does not care about you or want to help you with your problems.

The best thing that you can do when you are trying to read body language is to think about the person as a whole, not just if they are male or female.

Chapter 4- Learning To Control Your Own Body Language

Learning to control your body language is something that many people are interested in but think is too hard for them to do. However, simply becoming aware of your body language and paying attention to it is going to help you learn how to control it.

Why would you want to learn how to control your body language?

One of the reasons that many people want to learn how to control their body language is because they want to learn how to communicate better. If a person knows that by leaning forward, they are going to show that they are interested in what is being said, they are more likely to lean forward when they want to show that they are interested.

Another reason that some people want to learn how to control their body language is because they want to stop letting people read how they are feeling. For example, when I was growing up, learning how to read body language was something that everyone around me seemed to be doing.

This meant that I was not able to hide anything even when I didn't want people knowing what was going on with me or how I was feeling. I began learning about body language so that when I had a certain feeling, instead of using the automatic body language, I would do the exact opposite, ensuring that I was able to keep some of what I was feeling a secret.

Is it feasible to try and learn how to control your body language?

If you are communicating with someone that is familiar with body language, for example, someone who has read this book, you will find that you won't have much problem tricking them so to speak when you take control of your body language.

However, if you were, for example, speaking to an agent trained in reading body language, there are certain things that you would have no control over, such as how your pupils dilate. This means that you would not be able to trick this person simply by controlling the body language that you are able to.

If you want to begin taking control of your body language, the first thing that you have to do is learn how to relax your body when you are feeling any emotion. In order to do this, it is important for you to learn some deep breathing techniques.

Simply taking 10 deep breaths in and releasing them slowly is going to reduce a lot of the signs that you are feeling embarrassed, under pressure or even that you are stressed.

Not only is this a great way for you to get control of your body, but it is also going to ensure that you are able to take control of your emotions. When your emotions are out of control, you are not going to be able to control your body language.

Begin by paying attention to your body language. For example, did you know that when you are remembering an event that happened in the past, your eyes naturally look to the right? When you are telling a lie, your eyes naturally look to the left.

Try telling a lie while you are looking in the mirror, forcing your eyes to the right instead of the left. If you do not want someone to know that you are attracted to them, do not touch them or look them in the eyes.

If you do not want someone to know that you are nervous, you will want to make sure that you do not have a tell, such as wringing your hands or playing with your hair.

What this means is that you are going to have to spend some time focusing on your own body language. Another great benefit of this is that when you focus on your own body language, you will be more aware of how other people are using body language as well.

Let's move on to a few things that you can do to control your body language. You can begin with learning how to show that you are concentrating or thinking.

You can show that you are thinking or concentrating by crossing one arm over your chest and placing your other hand on your chin. If the thumb is pointed at a downward angle, and index finger is pointed up, it will signify that you are thinking.

If you want to show someone that you are interested, when you are in a formal situation such as an interview, you will want to sit up straight while looking directly at the person speaking. If you are speaking with a friend, or in a none formal situation, you do not have to worry about sitting up straight, but should instead, lean forward in order to show your interest.

In order to gain someone's trust, it is important that you have some type of physical contact with them. This can vary from a pat on the back to a gentle touch of their arm to a handshake in more formal situations.

You might find yourself in a situation where you want to appear alert and in control, such as walking down the street in a part of town that you are not comfortable in…

In order to appear as if you alert and paying attention to everything around you, it is important for you to first push your shoulders back while keeping your back straight and your head raised. You do not want to lower your head in this type of situation because this will make you appear to be less confident.

Moving on, I want to talk a little bit about how you can control your voice. As I stated earlier in this book, your voice can give away a lot about you if a person knows how to read it. Therefore, it is important for you to understand how to control it if you want to be able to communicate better and reduce the amount of emotion in it.

Begin by breathing from your belly. When most people breathe, they lift their shoulders as they inhale. Did you know that this is the wrong way to breathe? Not only is it healthier for you to breathe from your stomach, but it is going to help you control the emotion in your voice as well.

Take a deep breath, but instead of breathing as you normally would, as you inhale, expand your stomach, keeping your shoulders from moving. When you exhale, your stomach will go back to normal. Continue practicing until this type of breathing becomes natural to you.

The second thing that you want to work on is your posture. Did you know that when you do not practice proper posture, your breathing is constricted? Why is breathing so important? It is because the air that you breathe is literally a source of power for your voice.

Practice sitting up straight or standing up straight with your shoulders back and your head up. This will allow you to breathe properly, which means that you will be able to speak with more power.

If you want to show that you are in agreement with someone, try mirroring their actions, their facial expressions, and even their posture. If you pay attention to the people that you are talking to, what you will find is that if they like or agree with you, they are going to begin mirroring you.

You do not want to take this to the extreme and become annoying, however, mirroring small movements or facial expressions is going to help build great rapport with those that you are communicating with.

Another thing that you can do is learn how to control the tone of your voice. It is important when you are speaking that you try to keep your voice as low as possible. When people are nervous or when they are trying to hide something, or even when they are excited, they tend to use a much higher pitched voice.

However, those that speak in a lower tone are often considered more confident than those that have a higher pitched voice. It is important for you to focus on your voice because when a person does not feel confident, they tend to speak in a more childlike voice.

Many people speak very quickly when they are upset or nervous making it very difficult for people to understand them. Think about a news anchor. They speak at a steady pace, which ensures that everyone listening is able to hear what is being said. Make a point of slowing down when you are nervous or excited and you will be amazed at what a difference it makes.

One thing that will help you slow down a lot is if you enunciate your words. When people are nervous or excited, speaking quickly, they tend to leave off the last letter of some of the words that they are saying. This often leads to people tuning out what is being said.

You may find that recording yourself reading a few paragraphs will help you enunciate better. You will want to make sure that you are taking breaths at natural intervals, and focus on speaking slowly as well as clearly.

After you have recorded yourself speaking, it is time to play it back. It is completely normal to hate the sound of your own recorded voice, however, you will have to move past that in order to complete this exercise.

While you are listening to the recording, you will not only want to focus on the mistakes and make note of what needs changing but you will want to focus on the things that you like about the recording as well. You will be amazed at the quick changes that you will be able to make in the way that you speak, just by listening to a recording of yourself.

Finally, the last way that you can improve the way that you speak has nothing to do with your voice at all but your hands. In order to communicate better, using body language, it is important to involve your hands while you are speaking. Remember, most of our communication is done through non-verbal gestures. It is for this reason that it is important for you to use your body while you are communicating with others.

Besides all of these tips, the best thing that you can do in order to control your own body language is simply pay attention to the way other people use body language. Pay attention to how they move their face when they are expressing certain emotions, how they move their hands while they are speaking and even how they sit when they are listening to you speak.

Chapter 5- Different Culture, Different Meanings

As much as we would all love to believe that we can communicate with different cultures by using the same body language, it simply is not true. Just like different cultures speak different languages and have different beliefs, body language has different meanings across different cultures as well.

It is all but impossible for you to really understand all of the differences between all of the cultures when it comes to even more impossible for you to actually put the use of these different types of body language into action.

The fact is that if you tried to implement all of the different uses of body language, you would spend most of your time with your head down and your hands in your pockets because you would be afraid of offending one culture or another.

In North America, eye contact is something that is encouraged, because it shows that you are interested in the person that is speaking or that you are paying attention to what is being said. However, in the Middle East, while eye contact between two people of the same sex is considered something that shows trust when it occurs between two people of the opposite sex, it is considered something that is inappropriate.

When someone makes eye contact in Asian, Latin American, and African cultures, it is considered a challenge. In some cultures, women are not allowed to look at men when they are speaking, but instead are required to look down. In other cultures such as in Japan, looking someone in the eye is uncomfortable.

In the United States, we all know how important a handshake can be, however, in other cultures, a handshake is considered rude. In the Middle East, men are not to shake hands with women that are not part of their family and in South America, a handshake is usually a much warmer gesture than it is in the United States. When two people shake hands in South America, they do not only grip hands, but usually, the left hand will take hold of the other person's elbow and the handshake will last much longer than in the US.

Greetings are another huge difference across cultures when people are communicating. In the United States, we often say hello, however, in Japan, people will bow to each other and in Italy, they will kiss each other on the cheek.

If someone were to greet you in the US by kissing you on the cheek, chances are that you would interpret that as a romantic gesture whereas in Italy, it is the norm.

Many of us have what we call a bubble. It is our personal space, a place that we do not want other people entering and if they do, we will quickly move or even end the conversation with them. However, in other cultures, it is much more common for people to find themselves more up close and personal with those around them, even to the point of touching. Then there are other cultures which require even more space than we in The United States do.

When it comes to personal space, the way that a person feels about it is going to depend a lot on how they were raised. For example, I do not like for people to be close to me at all. In fact, while I do own a loveseat, I do not allow anyone to sit next to me on it because I feel like they are invading my personal space.

Along with personal space comes how we touch people. In some cultures such as the Latino culture, touching is encouraged however, there are many cultures in which touching is looked down upon. For example, there are some religions in which a man will only touch one woman his entire life, that woman being his wife. There are other cultures where you are never allowed to touch a person's head. What this means is that while you are out networking or meeting new people, it is probably best that you do not touch them, to ensure you do not offend them. At least until you get to know them better.

Small talk is another form of communication that we use and while it is not body language, it is important to understand the differences in cultures. For example, how many times have you simply asked someone how they were doing and they, without knowing you, gave you the full rundown of how terrible things were going in their life?

In some cultures, this would never happen as you would probably get a nod in response to your question if the question was acknowledged at all. However, in most cultures, small talk or asking someone how they are doing is looked down upon and should be avoided altogether.

Now that we have covered some of the cultural differences, let's focus a bit more on gestures. The meanings of different gestures vary widely across different cultures. Where in one culture a simple gesture may not hold much meaning, in another culture, it could be a huge insult.

One example of this would be the OK signal given by hand. While it is not common to use in the US, it is very common in Britain and signals that two people have come to an agreement. However, if you were to use this hand gesture in Brazil, it would be taken as an insult, much like flipping someone off in the US.

This gesture is also considered an insult in many other cultures such as Latin America, France, and even Australia.

Most of us know what the thumbs up means, we see it on social media all of the time, however, while it is accepted in the US as well as England, in other cultures it is considered a type of insult. Using this gesture in any area of the America's EXCEPT for the United States is considered a sexual insult.

The nodding of the head is something that many people do in the

United States because they want to show that they agree with the person that they are speaking with or that they are paying attention to what is being said. In the majority of the world, nodding the head means that you are agreeing with the speaker, however in Bulgaria, it means no.

While in the US, showing the soles of a one's feet is not something that many people think about, however, in some parts of the world, such as the Middle East, it is a gesture that means, "You are less than what I walk on."

There are many different ways that body language can be interpreted and of course this is not a complete list. If you are traveling abroad, it is important for you to do a bit of research so you are sure that you will not use body language that is found insulting.

Chapter 6- Body Language Myths

There are many myths that are associated with body language and I, like many others have fallen victim to these myths.

1. When a person avoids eye contact it means that they are lying or hiding something. This myth has been proven untrue time and time again, however, many people still stick to this belief. There are many people out there who are just not comfortable looking someone in the eyes. It may cause them to tear up because of the pain that they see in the person's eyes or it may make them feel as if the person is looking right through them. No matter the reason, not everyone likes to be looked in the eye. If you are one of these people, in order to avoid looking others in the eye, look at their forehead, at the space right between their eyes.

2. Everyone uses the same body language. We have already discussed the difference in men and women and the body language that they use, but it is also important to understand that every single person is different and they will use different body language in different ways. For example, some body language experts will teach you that if a person touches their neck while they are talking, they are lying. However, some people touch their neck when they are thinking or even when they are nervous. This does not take into account that a person may actually need to scratch their neck while they are speaking to you.

3. You can determine what a person is thinking based on a single movement. I mentioned this earlier, how it is important for you to pay attention to all of the signals that the person is giving you as well as the situation around you.

An example being that if a person crosses their arms, it does not mean that they are distancing themselves from you. If you really want to be able to read body language, you need to pay attention to everything that is going on, not just the one gesture.

4. People who are fidgeting are trying to hide something. This should be obvious. When people are focused on what is being said or they are trying to remember it for future use, they tend to fidget or even doodle on a sheet of paper. People who are deep in thought tend to fidget as well, without even noticing it.

5. People who are smiling are generally happy and truthful. Smiles are so easy to fake and if a person was raised to believe that they should smile all of the time, they can become really good at faking these smiles. Even salesmen use a good smile to get you to trust them and purchase the item they are selling. This does not mean they are always telling you the truth about the item.

Why is it important to understand that there are myths when it comes to reading body language? It is important because while learning about body language can be fascinating, it can also be quite confusing. You have to remember that you never want to assume anything.

It is important for you to remember that while you are learning how to read body language, you are not going to be able to read it overnight. While you may be able to pick up on one or two clues here and there, unless you learn how to pay attention to the entire situation, the environment and all of the different types of body language that you see people displaying you will never be able to really read body language.

One last tip before we end this book. If you want to learn how to read body language, I suggest that you take a small pocket notebook and write down some of the common body language signals that you want to watch for. For example, if you are wanting to understand if someone is romantically interested in you, write down some of the common signs.

Then, before you interact with that person, read over the signs and pay close attention to your interaction.

Many times, when we are interacting with someone that we are attracted to, we are not focusing on what is actually happening, then when we look back on it, we are not sure if what we believed happened is actually what happened.

Make small notes in your mind as to how the person touches you and the type of body language that they are using so that you can spend time really focusing on interpreting the situation later.

Conclusion-

Most of the time when people think of body language, they think of gestures that people use and have no hopes of ever being able to understand them. However, with the information that you have learned in this book, you will now be able to understand what people really are communicating to you.

Now you don't have to wonder about how someone feels about you or if they are being honest with you. All you have to do is pay attention to the small movements that they are making with their face or their body.

If you really want to become great at learning how to read body language, become what is known as a people watcher. Sit in the park, not listening in on people's conversations but just observing their body language and try to determine what they are expressing.

Understanding how to read body language is not only going to help you when it comes to finding out if someone is attracted to you, but it is going to help you in every area of your life. You are going to be able to tell if someone is being truthful, how your comments make them feel and if they are open to your ideas.

You will no longer have to wonder how a meeting went or if you made a good impression during an interview because you are going to be able to read the body language of the people you are communicating with and understand how they feel about you.

This is also going to allow you to change the way you approach different people. Because you are going to be able to tell how open a person is to what you are saying, if you find that you say something that makes them feel uncomfortable or sensitive, you will be able to change the way you are communicating with them.

Body language plays a role in every part of our lives every single day and it is for that reason that we should learn how to read it. I hope that the information that you have learned in this book has gotten you one step closer to understanding body language.

Thank you again for downloading this book!

I hope this book was able to help you to understand how body language affects us and also enjoyed the book!

The next step is to be sure that you fully understand the information, also apply it and read it as frequently as necessary.

Finally, if you enjoyed this book, then I'd like to ask you for a favour, would you be kind enough to leave a review for this book on Amazon? It'd be greatly appreciated!

If you enjoyed the the this book check out other releases that you might like:

Social Anxiety: Guide to Overcome Shyness, Shame, Social Phobia and to Understand How to Help Yourself to Achieve Social Freedom

Mobile Apps: 10 Smartphone Apps That Will Earn You Money While Walking